Entertaining
A Dog's World

Entertaining
A Dog's World

Asia Upward

NEW HOLLAND

Contents

*Dedicated to the dogs of the world
and the people who love them.*

Entreés

Bear's Crackers

Ingredients

50 g (1.7 oz) cup sunflower seeds

50 g (1.7 oz) pumpkin kernels

50 g (1.7 oz) golden flaxseed meal

50 g (1.7 oz) tapioca flour

25 g (1 oz) chia seeds

Fresh rosemary

1 egg

60 ml (2 fl oz) of water

1 teaspoon apple cider vinegar

Directions

In a food processor, add together all of the dry ingredients and blend until they are a fairly fine consistency.

Add in the egg, water and apple cider vinegar and mix again until you get dough like consistency.

Place the dough on a piece of baking paper and press it down with your hands. Finely chop some of the rosemary and sprinkle it over the top.

Place a second piece of baking paper over the top of the dough and use a rolling pin to roll it out until it is about 5 mm (¼ in) thick. Remove the top piece of paper and use a pizza cutter to cut the crackers into the desired shapes. Place the cut pieces onto a baking tray that is lined with baking paper.

Bake for 15 minutes on both sides or until golden.

Nori Wrapped Canapés

Ingredients

100 g (3.5 oz) cup brown rice

1 egg

95 g (3 oz) tin of salmon

1 small carrot, sliced

1 small cucumber, sliced

125 ml (4 fl oz) sunflower oil

Yaki Nori seaweed sushi sheets

Directions

Cook the brown rice as per the instructions on the packet and leave to cool, then mix in the egg.

Place cling wrap across a small muffin tin and push the rice mixture firmly into the muffin spaces and leave in fridge to set for 30 minutes.

In a saucepan, heat the sunflower oil.

Pop the rice balls out of the muffin tin and fry in the saucepan until golden brown. Drain excess oil off on paper towels

Using a fork, mash up the tinned salmon chunks.

Slice the carrot and cucumber into thin slices.

Cut the Nori sheet into 2 cm (¾ in) strips.

Stack the salmon onto the rice. Place the carrot and cucumber on top, then wrap the Nori sheet around it, using a small amount of water on the edges to make them stick.

Egg Canapé

Ingredients

4 eggs

95 g (3 oz) tin of salmon

1 tablespoon cottage cheese

Caviar of your choice

Fresh dill

Directions

Boil the eggs in a saucepan and once cooked cut them in half, removing the yolk to a separate bowl.

Mix together the salmon, egg yolks and cottage cheese.

Spoon the mixture back into the egg whites and garnish with caviar and fresh dill to serve.

Tuna and Cucumber Canapé

Ingredients

1 medium cucumber, sliced

95 g (3 oz) can of tuna in oil

Salmon roe caviar

Fresh dill, to garnish

Directions

Peel cucumber and cut into pieces about 5 mm (0.2 in) thick.

Put the tuna in a bowl and mash it up.

Place the tuna on the cucumber slices.

Top with salmon roe caviar and fresh dill.

Apple Sliders

Ingredients

1 red apple, washed

1 medium banana

4 tablespoons natural peanut butter with no salt

Fresh mint leaves, to garnish

Directions

Slice the apple into rounds and lay flat on a serving plate.

Slice the banana in half lengthways, and then half again, and place on top of the apple slices.

Spoon 1 tablespoon of peanut butter over the top of the banana.

Garnish with fresh mint to serve.

Crown Jewel Canapé

Ingredients

Bear's crackers
(see page 10)

1 medium sweet potato, mashed

300–400 g (11–14 oz) chicken
breast

2 small carrots, cut into ribbons

Gold caviar

Directions

Use a fine slicer or mandolin to cut the carrots into thin ribbons.

Roll up the carrot ribbons and use a toothpick to hold them in place. Add them to ice water and leave in the freezer overnight.

Steam sweet potato for 15–17 minutes, or until tender.

Boil the chicken breast until cooked through completely.

Use a food processor to mash up the sweet potato with the chicken.

Spoon the sweet potato mixture onto the Bear's crackers.

Take the carrots out of water and remove the toothpick.

You can loosen them up and add them to the top of the sweet potato.

Garnish with gold caviar to serve.

Fish Jerky

Ingredients

200 g (7 oz) salmon fillets, sliced

Fresh rosemary, to garnish

Directions

Heat oven to 160°C (325°F).

Slice the salmon fillets into bite-size strips.

Place the strips onto baking paper lined baking tray.

Cook for 1 ½ hours until dry and leave in oven to cool.

Garnish with fresh rosemary to serve.

Mini Salmon Frittata

Ingredients

8 eggs

40 g (1½ oz) dill

110 g (4 oz) salmon

Broccolini

60 ml (2fl oz) coconut milk

Directions

Prheat oven to 180 °C (350°F).

Whisk together the eggs, coconut milk and fresh dill.

Grease the muffin tin and line with baking paper.

Place a few small broccolini heads into the muffin tin.

Lightly steam the salmon for 2 minutes.

Place the small chunks of salmon into the muffin tin and pour the egg mixture over the top.

Bake for 20 minutes or until they begin to turn golden brown.

Meatballs

Ingredients

500 g (17 oz) lean mince

1 small carrot, grated

½ small pumpkin, grated (in equal amount to the carrot)

1 sprig fresh rosemary

1 egg

60 ml (2 fl oz) sunflower oil

Yogurt, for garnish

Parsley, for garnish

Sesame seeds, for garnish

Directions

Preheat oven to 180 ° C (350°F).

Add together the mince, carrot, pumpkin, rosemary and egg and mix well until it forms a thick mixture.

Roll the mixture into balls and place onto a lightly greased baking tray.

Cook for 35 minutes or until cooked through.

Garnish the meatballs with yogurt, parsley and sesame seeds to serve.

Grilled Pear Canapés

Ingredients

Bear's crackers (see page 10)

300 g (10.5 oz) cottage cheese

1 pear, sliced

2 tablespoons pepitas, finely chopped

Directions

On a grill, lighly cook the pear slices for 1–2 minutes on each side.

Spoon a teaspoon of cottage cheese onto each bear cracker and top with a pear slice.

Garnish with pepitas to serve.

Flaxseed Crisp Bread

Ingredients

80 g (2.8 oz) flaxseed

100 g (3.5 oz) golden flaxseed meal

1 egg

1 teaspoon apple cider vinegar

Directions

Preheat oven to 180 °C (350°F).

Mix together all ingredients, and roll the mixture out onto baking paper using your hands.

Place a piece of baking paper over the top of the flattened mix and use a rolling pin to roll it out to the desired thickness.

Use a cookie cutter to cut them into desired shape.

Place them on a baking paper lined tray and bake for 20 minutes, or until they are crisp.

Prawn and Pea Canapé

Ingredients

175 g (6 oz) prawns, peeled

125 g (4.5 oz) frozen green peas, mashed

Flaxseed crisp breads (see page 35)

Directions

Boil the peas for 2–3 minutes, or until cooked through, then mash.

Spoon the pea mash onto the crisp bread.

Place one peeled prawn on top of each.

Veal Schnitzel with Pear Slaw

Ingredients

150–200 g (5–7 oz) veal schnitzel

1 egg

75 g (3 oz) ground golden flax-seed

75 ml (3 fl oz) sunflower oil

1 pear, julienned

Fresh dill, finely chopped

Directions

Slice the veal into small pieces.

Whisk the egg well and set aside.

Pour the ground golden flaxseed into a seperate bowl.

Roll each slice of veal in the egg, and then in the flaxseed and set aside.

Heat sunflower oil in a pan over medium heat.

Once hot, add in the veal and cook until golden and crunchy on both sides.

Garnish with julienned pear and dill to serve.

Kale Chips with Crispy Bacon

Ingredients

1 bunch kale

1 medium bacon rasher, fat removed

1 teaspoon coconut oil

Directions

Heat oven to 180 °C (350°F).

Tear the kale into small, chip size pieces.

Finely chop the bacon and cook it in a pan until golden brown.

Heat up the coconut oil and pour the oil over the kale leaves, mixing well.

Place the kale leaves on a baking tray lined with baking paper.

Sprinkle the bacon bits over the top of the kale leaves and bake for 10 minutes, or until crunchy.

Veal Wrapped Asparagus Spears

Ingredients

6 asparagus spears

100–150g (3–5 oz) veal, sliced thinly

75 ml (3 fl oz) sunflower oil

Sesame seeds, to garnish

Parsley, chopped, to garnish

200 g (7 oz) tzatziki

Directions

Preheat oven to 190 °C (375°F).

Wrap the veal around the asparagus and hold them it place with a toothpick.

Line a baking tray with aluminum foil and grease with sunflower oil.

Place the asparagus onto the foil and lightly paint them with the remaining sunflower oil.

Bake for 20 minutes or until veal is cooked completely through.

Garnish with sesame seeds and parsley and a side of tzatziki.

Prawn Cocktail

Ingredients

150–200 g (5–7 oz) prawns,
peeled and deveined

1 bunch kale, leaves torn

Directions

In a glass, place a handful of kale leaves and top with peeled prawns.

Mains

Beef Carpaccio with Pesto

Ingredients

250–300 g (9–10.5 oz) rib eye beef steak

30 g (1 oz) basil leaves

150 g (5 oz) pepitas

120 ml (4 oz) sunflower oil, plus extra for meat coating

Directions

Lightly coat the meat on both sides with sunflower oil.

Heat your grill and cook beef for 2 minutes on each side, then leave to rest.

In a food processor, mix together the basil leaves, pepitas and 120 ml (4 oz) of sunflower oil to create the pesto.

Finely slice your beef and layer it on a plate.

Serve with the pesto mix as a side garnish.

Pea and Ham Soup

Ingredients

300g (11 oz) split peas

1 small ham hock

300 g (11 oz) frozen peas

1 small bunch mint, leaves torn

Directions

Preheat oven to 180°C (350°F).

In an ovenproof pot, place the ham hock and split peas, and fill with enough water to cover the ham hock completely.

Place the pot in the oven and cook for 1 hour, then stir.

Cook for another hour, adding extra water if needed.

Take the ham hock out of the pot and pull the meat off the bone.

Steam the frozen peas and add them into the split peas and blend.

Add the meat back to the pea mix and garnish with fresh mint leaves and ham hock meat to serve.

Rosemary Lamb Spears

Ingredients

500 g (17 oz) lamb mince

½ teaspoon turmeric

1 egg

5 thick, long sprigs of rosemary

1 tablespoon sunflower oil

100 g (3.5 oz) natural yogurt

1 small bunch mint, finely chopped

1 small cucumber, finely sliced

Directions

Prepare the rosemary by pulling the bottom leaves from the rosemary sprigs.

In a bowl, combine the lamb mince, tumeric, egg and rosemary leaves, and mix well.

Roll the meat mixture in balls around the rosemary sprigs.

In a pan, heat sunflower oil and cook the meatballs on the sprigs.

Remove the spears and let rest on paper towels to drain excess oil.

Make some tzatziki dipping sauce by mixing together yogurt, mint and cucumber.

Lemongrass and Chicken Spears

Ingredients

200 g (7 oz) chicken mince

1 ½ tablespoon coconut flour

1 small zucchini (courgette), grated

½ teaspoon ginger

6 lemongrass skewers

75 ml (3 fl oz) sunflower oil

Directions

Preheat oven to 180°C (350°F).

Mix together mince, flour, zucchini, ginger in a bowl and leave in the fridge to rest for an hour.

Cut the lemongrass in half and use a rolling pin to gently roll over one end to release the lemongrass flavour.

Roll the mince mixture around the side of the newly formed lemongrass skewer.

Line a baking tray with foil and grease with sunflower oil.

Place the chicken skewers on to the foil and bake for 35 minutes or until golden brown.

Zucchini Wraps

Ingredients

500 g (17 oz) pork mince

1 medium zucchini (courgette),
cut into ribbons

1 tablespoon cottage cheese

75 ml (3 fl oz) sunflower oil

Directions

Heat oven to 180°C (350°F).

In a bowl, combine the mince with cottage cheese and mix well.

Cut the zucchini into ribbons.

Take a small amount of the pork mixture and roll the zucchini ribbon around the mixture.

Hold the wrap in place with a toothpick.

Line a baking tray with foil and lightly grease with sunflower oil.

Place the zucchini rolls on the tray, paint with sunflower oil and bake for 35 minutes.

Remove toothpick and serve.

Zucchini Sliders

Ingredients

1 medium zucchini (courgette), sliced

200 g (7 oz) beef eye fillet

200 g (7 oz) frozen peas

½ bunch of basil, leaves removed

75 g (3 oz) pepitas, extra for garnish

75 ml (3 fl oz) sunflower oil

Directions

Slice the zucchini and lightly grill.

Boil the frozen peas until cooked, and then mash.

Grill the beef eye fillet for a couple of minutes on each side, leave to rest and thinly slice.

Make pesto by adding together the basil, 75 ml (3 fl oz) of sunflower oil and 75 g (3 oz) of peptitas and blend.

Stack the pea mash onto the zucchini slices, top with beef slices and drizzle with pesto.

Sprinkle with some extra pepitas to serve.

Stuffed Chicken

Ingredients

350–400 g (12–14 oz) chicken breast, thinly sliced

½ small sweet potato, chopped

200 g (7 oz) pork mince

1 small bunch parsley, chopped

Directions

Heat oven to 180°C (350°F).

Chop sweet potato into small pieces and boil until soft.

Add sweet potato, pork mince and parsley together and mix well.

Roll the chicken breast around the mince mixture and use toothpicks to hold them in place.

Bake in an ovenproof dish for 45 minutes.

Slice and serve.

Chicken Curry

Ingredients

300–400 g (11–14 oz) chicken breast, chopped

1 small sweet potato, chopped

1 small carrot, chopped

1 small zucchini (courgette), chopped

250 g (9 0z) tin of light coconut milk

1 tablespoon sunflower oil

150 ml (5 fl oz) water

150 g (5 oz) brown rice, for serving

Directions

Chop chicken into bite size pieces.

Heat sunflower oil in a saucepan and brown chicken lightly.

Chop the sweet potato, carrot and zucchini into small pieces and add to chicken.

Cook in pan for 3 minutes, then add in the tin of coconut milk and water to the saucepan and simmer for 40 minutes.

Let curry cool and serve over brown rice.

Desserts

Berry Daiquiri

Ingredients

200 g (8 oz) frozen berries

1 medium banana

240 ml (8 fl oz) water

Directions

Blend together the frozen berries, banana and water.

Garnish with a whole strawberry to serve.

Apple Fritters

Ingredients

3 medium apples

60 ml (2 fl oz) maple syrup

25 g (1 oz) coconut flour

25 g (1 oz) arrowroot flour

60 ml (2 fl oz) coconut milk

sunflower oil

Directions

Remove the apple core and cut apple into slices.

In a bowl, add together the maple syrup, flour, and milk to create a batter.

Heat sunflower oil in a frypan.

Coat the apple slices with batter and add into the frying pan to cook.

Once golden, remove from pan, drain the excess oil out on baking paper and allow to cool before serving.

Strawberry Shortcake

Ingredients

100 g (3 oz) coconut flour

1 teaspoon baking powder

60 ml (2 fl oz) maple syrup

1 teaspoon cinnamon

240 ml (8 fl oz) almond milk

2 eggs

120 ml (4 fl oz) sunflower oil

100 g (3 oz) toasted coconut

Directions

Heat oven to 180°C (350°F).

Mix together the coconut flour, baking powder, maple syrup, cinnamon, almond milk, eggs and sunflower oil.

Grease a mini muffin tin and spoon mixture into the tin.

Bake for 20 minutes or until just golden brown.

For icing, mix together the yogurt with 1 teaspoon of coconut flour.

Scoop 1 tablespoon of icing onto each shortcake and garnish with strawberry halves and toasted coconut to serve.

Fruit Medley Canapé

Ingredients

1 small rockmelon, sliced

200g (7 oz) cottage cheese

1 punnet strawberries, halved

Directions

Slice the rockmelon and strawberries.

Scoop a spoonful of cottage cheese on top of each slice of rockmelon.

Top with a strawberry half.

Animal SOS Sri Lanka

Animal SOS Sri Lanka is a charity dedicated to alleviating the suffering of street animals in Sri Lanka. Kim Cooling, a British tourist who had visited the island, was so moved by the heartbreaking plight of stray animals, that she founded the Animal SOS Sri Lanka charity to help. The charity has a no-kill policy, and a 4 acre free roaming animal sanctuary in the south of the island where they currently care for over 700 destitute cats and dogs, many nursed back to health from serious diseases and horrific injuries.

They are operational 365 days a year and have an on-site veterinary clinic where they employ a resident vet as well as other local staff to help care for the sanctuary animals. They offer refuge, rehabilitation, local feeding and life saving veterinary care for sick, injured and starving strays. They also operate an empowering animal adoption program. Animal SOS Sri Lanka provide weekly outreach programs in the local villages where they conduct health checks, sterilize and vaccinate cats and dogs against rabies, provide worming treatments, and treat wounds, infections and skin conditions. Animal SOS Sri Lanka provide animal welfare educational materials, collars and leads to local communities so as to prevent painful neck injuries caused by collar tethering with ropes and wire.

The amazing work done by Animal SOS Sri Lanka benefits not only the animals, but also the local human population, as it works towards creating a safer, healthier environment for all. Animal SOS Sri Lanka feeds around 800 animals each day and the running costs are mounting. They desperately need finanical assistance to continue their great work. You can help create happier, healthier lives for stray animals through www.animalsos-sl.com.

Animal SOS Sri Lanka is an outstanding charity. The work they do to help animals that have otherwise been abandoned is without parallel, and because of this I will continue to support them by raising awareness and donating a portion of the royalties from *Entertaining A Dog's World*.

Asia Upward

Meet the Models

Meet the Models

Important Disclaimer

It is recommended that you always consult your vet on the dietary requirements of your dog before commencing a new diet.

Credits

Photography and recipes: Asia Upward

Food Styling: Kirsty Bryson

Props: The Prop Dispensary

Acknowledgements

I would like to thank the following for their contributions to the book:

All the dog owners: Kirsty Bryson, Bronwyn LeGrice, Tom LeGrice, Jason McIntyre, Nadine Kiss, Aaron Harris, Kimberley Duband, Fleur Duband, Cathy Stirling, Leah Carroll, Verity Adams, Mandy Emery, Hewett Family, Jonathan Jones, Gurwinder Singh, Kylie Carnaffan

Pet Home Stay (www.pethomestay.com.au) who helped find me some amazing models.

I would like to thank my dog, Bear, who is always happy to offer his services as a recipe approver.

Join A Dog's World on Instagram @a.dogs.world for further information about Animal SOS Sri Lanka.

Index

First published in 2015 by New Holland Publishers Pty Ltd

London • Sydney • Auckland

The Chandlery Unit 009 50 Westminster Bridge Road London SE1 7QY United Kingdom
1/66 Gibbes Street Chatswood NSW 2067 Australia
5/39 Woodside Ave Northcote, Auckland 0627

www.newhollandpublishers.com

A record of this book is held at the British Library and the National Library of Australia.

ISBN: 9781742577982

Managing Director: Fiona Schultz
Publisher: Diane Ward
Project Editor: Jessica McNamara
Designer: Kathie Baxter Eastway
Production Director: Olga Dementiev
Printer: Toppan Leefung Printing Limited
10 9 8 7 6 5 4 3 2 1

Keep up with New Holland Publishers on Facebook
www.facebook.com/NewHollandPublishers